The Shawnise Chantell Story

God Within The Lily
The Death and Resurrection of Me

The Shawnise Chantell Story

God Within The Lily
The Death and Resurrection of Me

Shawnise Chantell

Copyright © 2022. Shawnise Chantell. All rights reserved.

The Shawnise Chantell Story is based on the author's recollection.

This book or any portion thereof may not be reproduced or used in any manner whatsoever without the express written permission of the author and publisher except for the use of brief quotations in a book review.

Printed in the United States of America.

ISBN:

Paperback 978-1-951883-75-1

Hardback: 978-1-951883-85-0

eBook: 978-1-951883-84-3

Library of Congress: 2022904911

Butterfly Typeface Publishing

PO Box 56193

Little Rock AR 72215

Dedication

God within the Lily is dedicated to those who left an imprint on my heart during my time of sickness and recovery. I am forever grateful for God's grace, mercy, and faithfulness. When I needed light in the darkness I put my faith in Him – my Miracle Worker, and Lily in The Valley.

To my parents, siblings, children, aunts and cousins, I also dedicate this book to you. Your love, strength, scarifies, thoughts, prayers, and acts of kindness are all appreciated. You are the epitome of family. There is an intimate place in my heart that is filled with so much gratitude.

To my super heroic mommies who bring life into this world: queens, may your pain, scars, love, and sacrifice never go unnoticed.

To my super dads, know that you too are appreciated!

I look up to the mountains — does my health come from there?
My help comes from the Lord, who made heaven and earth!"

Psalm 121: 1-2 (NLT)

Table of Contents

Introduction 23

Chapter One: Resiliency 27

Chapter Two: Dates to Remember 33

    Dates to Remember Photos 42

Chapter Three: Spiritual Ascension 47

Chapter Four: Craziness 53

Photo Gallery 59

Chapter Five: Remembrance 69

Chapter Six: God's Blessings 73

Chapter Seven: Faith and Family 81

Chapter Eight: My Altered Life 89

Chapter Nine: Recovery 95

Chapter Ten: God's Provisions 101

Conclusion: Here's What Happened 109

About the Author 115

A Note from the Publisher 121

Journal 135

Praise for God Within the Lily 159

Foreword

I met Ms. Shawnise Chantell January of 2020.

My first impression was that she was fearful and hesitant.

Her father told me of her encounter with the medical profession. He too was worried and fearful that she wouldn't make it.

After speaking to Ms. Shawnise for an hour and forty minutes, I understood why she shies away from medical professionals. Her near-death experience and ability to come back to tell this beautiful, yet surreal experience left me (a mental health provider) marveled.

Ms. Shawnise's encounter was told as if it came from a dream or a well written novel, however, this was her experience.

My first thought was, "This is traumatic. What can I do to help her?"

Because of her experience, she was fearful of going to sleep and would therefore take frequent and brief naps during the day.

When I met her, she had just gotten a pacemaker a month prior. After telling me about the pacemaker and being fearful of being shocked I learned of her apprehension.

I suggested medications that were helpful for Post-Traumatic Stress Disorder (PTSD) patients but again she was apprehensive. I worked cohesively with another counselor to guide Ms. Shawnise through the process. But I realized, she continued to be unable to move past her experience.

Then I suggested she write about her experience.

"Just start writing," I encouraged. "And watch how the story will flow. You'll be able to release some of your anguish."

Time passed and after countless session hours, she showed up one day with exciting news:

"You won't believe this," she began. "I have been writing a book and even did a podcast about my near-death experience!"

I was amazed that she had trusted me, believed in my work and allowed herself to be vulnerable. Shawnise put herself through the test to tell her testimony and is now on her way to recovery.

The journey isn't over, but she can begin to live again.

One thing she said to me was, "I don't like these scars or the body I'm in."

"This is new," I reminded her. "And you will either adapt or stay stagnant. Your scars are a reminder that you're on a new journey. We are all a vessel for a purpose while we're here on earth. Your spirit has been placed in this temporary, scared vessel to tell of a beautiful encounter with your Creator."

Working with Ms. Shawnise has helped me to see myself as a vessel - serving His purpose and helping others.

Thank you, Ms. Shawnise, for allowing me to share with the world how therapy can help overcome trauma.

Dahlia Distin

DNPs PMHNP CNP APRN

Acknowledgments

To my children:

First-born Alexis Keairra - my Lexi pooh: I know that being 16 and taking care of your younger sibling Naomi Grace (who was just 11 months old at the time) for 2 ½ months while I was hospitalized was a difficult task. The shoes you wore were hard, but you did an excellent job baby girl! Your name, Alexis, which means "Helper," describes you perfectly. You have a giving heart, you are unique, bold, beautiful, and wonderfully made. You have a raspy, singing voice of an angel and I hope you one day realize it's a special gift from God.

Second-born, Naomi Grace, my mini me and lioness twin: We spent your first birthday celebration apart, but you stayed very close in my heart! I asked your auntie Tia to stand in my place and take you on a shopping spree. I knew during your shopping spree, you would pick out something musical because you love putting on a show, bringing so much joy and laughter. Your smile is infectious to everyone who knows you. Our princess Jasmine photo shoot for your second birthday was very special. Your name means "Pleasantness". You are peaceful, bring great beauty, very wise, a genius and the world will one day see your greatness. Follow your heart, always pray, always be respectful and your debut and center stage moment will be spectacular.

My last-born Kensi Elise: Fom the first moment I held you I knew you were my miracle child. When my health declined after your delivery, I fought hard to get back to you so I could give you my love, warm hugs and kisses, and show you everything that I had planned for us during your first few months of life. Kensi, your name means a "fighter." Without knowing, you gave me strength. I love seeing you grow! You're a little chocolate drop, mini-Laila Ali, and your essence is breathless! I love that you are wittingly smart, amazing, hilarious, sassy, super sweet after my heart and I can't take my eyes off of you. You will achieve anything you set your mind to! **Mommy loves you all forever and always!**

To my Mommy Dearest: your love and comfort I could never repay but I will never stop thanking you for giving me life and for being by my side every step of the way. You gave my sister and I your best, a good life! Your voice, your touch and your hugs got me through many tough days. When I had a thought of giving up, you reminded me of my faith in God and belief that death wasn't an option for me. When I was back in a baby state, and all of my womanly dignity was lost, you never made me feel like a burden! You always made sure that I would try to eat something. One thing is for sure, my hospital room stayed well-kept, and I was fresh. You are my best friend and the best mommy in the world. Your heart is angelic. May God enrich you always. Sistergirl you are a warrior! **I love you, Mom!**

To my Daddy, Papa P - the heart of a giant: You are my company keeper. Just thinking about how much you have done to nurse me back to good health gives me happy tears and gratitude. From the long nights in the hospital to the responsibility of taking care of me. You were my caretaker and I thank you for keeping your promise. You were my everyday voice when I couldn't speak. Keeping track of my appointments, medical supplies, medications, ensuring that my life vest, wound vac, and IV pump stayed working properly, and coordinating with my home health nurse was an overwhelming task but you did it with ease. You helped me to gain the strength to eat! Daddy you are my right-hand man and a one-of-a-kind dad! You are my super dad! **Love always your sweet pea.**

To my praying Grandma Lewis: Your prayers seem to always reach the ears of God. You are an example of a faithful servant. I can always count on you and your wisdom. Thank you for Always teaching me to rely on God's word - Psalms 121. It took endurance and patience, but I meditated on Psalms 121 often throughout my sickness. **Thanks Grandma I love you.**

To my sister Latia, my ace boon coon! My sister's keeper: I am so proud of you. Your gift of caring for others will take you very far because you put so much love into what you do. The medical field fits your gifts very well. The detailed care you gave me was remarkable. Thanks for always making me feel beautiful by doing my makeup and hair in the hospital. I appreciate you for putting your nursing career on hold to help be there for me, Alexis, and Naomi. I can't imagine how my sickness really affected you. I am sure I worked your nerves, lol. We worship together, we cry together, we laugh together, we sang together. I also appreciate you for the responsibility of taking my vitals at home, flushing my IV line as necessary, and changing my wound dressings. You are the epitome of selflessness and a wonderful big sister. You uplifted my spirits many days in the hospital and always kept me rooted. You give me a balance between love and tough love, and I appreciate you for that. You helped me learn to rely on my own strength and made me realize my mind and body was stronger than my circumstances. You are my sister, and my friend. **I Love You chic!**

To my Auntie Brenda and Auntie Ellamae: I am truly blessed to have the both of you. You are my spiritual mommies! I didn't have to worry about nothing in the hospital because you were my voice. You were my advocates alongside my mom. I looked forward to your visits. Thank you for spending so much time with me ensuring that I was ok. On my birthday, when I'd gotten the horrible news about my health status, I was sad and frighten and it sucked not enjoying my birthday as I'd hoped. But I will never forget the beautiful surprise birthday balloons you gave me to brighten my day. There's a special place in my heart for both of you! **I love my Aunties!**

To my cousin Steven: Thank you for always showing up on time to check on me in the hospital and keeping me company. I enjoyed our real-life conversations. **I am so blessed to have a cousin like you!**

To my best friends, Chauna and Bobbie: Thanks for always reaching out to me. I love you ladies!

To my previous work family at Arkansas Heart Hospital Clinic. Thank you for sending me a beautiful flower arrangement while I was in the hospital. It was nice seeing the flowers bloom.

To Norris, Mike and Kevin, I appreciate you guys as well.

To Cruz, thank you for showing me the beach for the first-time. I finally know what it's like to relax with my feet in the sand while hearing the music of the waves. The view was paradise and put a lot of things in my life in good perspective. Thank you for all things you do so I can focus on writing and inspiring others!

To the doctors and nurses who worked on me tirelessly for 20 minutes during my cardiac arrest. I thank you from the bottom of my heart for not giving up and for bringing me back to my girls. I thank God who sent me a team of Angels: family, Surgical Team, Hospitals, Cardiologists, Heart Transplant Team, Pulmonary Team, Infectious disease, Chaplin, GI Team, Nephrologist, Home Health Nurse, Counselor and Psychiatrist.

To my late Grandpa Davis and Aunt Rita. Thank you both for your inspiring memories. I miss both of you so much. Until we meet again, my spiritual angels in heaven, rest in love.

Finally, but never the least, thank you Iris M. Williams (Butterfly Typeface Publishing) for driving, leading, and guiding my story to its greatness! I appreciate your anointed touch, knowledge, and expertise! Thank you for always being available to collaborate on ideas and for going the extra mile. Thank you for welcoming me to your family and community of writers.

Photo 1 Author Shawnise Chantell

Photo 2 Author Shawnise Chantell

Introduction

For I know the plans I have for you," says the Lord.
"They are plans for good and not for disaster,
to give you a future and a hope."
Jeremiah 29:11(NLT)

Who Am I?

I am Shawnise Chantell. In 2019, at the age of 34, I experienced a 20 minute, near death, out-of-body experience.

I had just given birth to beautiful baby girl and now that I was a mother of three, I decided my family was complete. I opted for a tubal ligation.

From all I knew, a tubal ligation was a simple and complication free experience. However, for me, it was the beginning of a 54-day hospital stay.

The tubal ligation led to a perforated bowel which ultimately led to physical and mental challenges.

My Scars

I have scars that are not that pretty. In fact, they are pretty ugly. However, I embrace them because they remind me every day just how close I came to being gone forever.

Why am I telling you this?

I am grateful that God spared my life.

My scars have shown me a new path; one that I am blessed to share with the world.

Telling my story has proven to be therapeutic. Through sharing, I am able to connect, motivate, and be a source of hope to others who may have shared similar experiences.

Faith

Although this experience tested my faith like never before, I kept going. I always knew I had faith but professing it and living it proved to be two totally different things.

My story – what I endured, how I overcame and what living by faith looks like - is not a story for me to keep. My story was pre-determined to be shared with the world!

Looking back, I can see God's plan for my life extended into a future that I never envisioned.

God Within the Lily

Chapter One: Resiliency

"My mission in life is not merely to survive, but to thrive; and to do so with some passion, some compassion, some humor, and some style."
Dr. Maya Angelou

Overcoming Childhood Struggles

Faith in God was something I feel I had to develop early in life.

As a child, I struggled with fitting in because of a speech impediment.

"Hey, Shawnise. Tell us about your weekend," Gloria said in a sing-song voice that brought tears to my eyes right away.

She looks at me, waiting for my response. I knew I had to say something, I wanted to say something like *hi* or *hello*. But her obvious grin at my muteness paralyzed my words. My mouth began to open but I couldn't spit the words out to just say, "Hey Gloria."

In fact, in order to get the words to move past my lips, I forced myself to smile big to break the silence. THEN the words began to flow.

"Hh-e-ey, G G gloria." I struggled just to say the simplest of things.

Gloria's teasing became fuel that lit a fire in me. With practice and persistence, I learned how to speak in a way that was less triggering for my speech impediment. Music and writing poems gave me an outlet for expression that focused more on my thoughts and feelings and less on my inability to pronounce them.

Over the years, I not only overcame the stuttering, but pushed pass learning disabilities and graduated high school, technical college, and later medical school.

Catalyst for Change

When we are going through things, we never stop to think of them as being for our good. But turns out they are if we take the time to search for the lesson.

I lost loved ones, endured childhood molestation, teen pregnancy, threats of homelessness, and divorce. While those things were devastating, they were only precursors for what I consider an ultimate test of faith.

A brush with death can have that effect!

Motherhood

I gave birth at the ages of 16, 32 and 33. The first two times I was able to bring new life into the world without any complications for my babies or myself.

After the birth of my first two children, my health was fine and after a short time, I bounced back to a normal, active lifestyle: Jumping out of airplanes, climbing mountains, traveling, and living my best life.

I loved life and loved being a mom.

I never dreamed being a mom would threaten my existence! My life changed forever in ways I didn't intend or welcome.

Change in Plans

After the delivery of my third daughter, I had definite plans for my life:

I was going to return to my dream job at the Arkansas Heart Hospital and continue my studies at the University of Arkansas for Medical Sciences. The goal was a Bachelor of Science in Health Information Technology.

I was going to return home with my newborn.

I was going to care for all three of my daughters.

I was going to care for me.

But things didn't go as planned:

Work and school were out of the question.

My newborn was sent to live with next-of-kin for nearly six months while I was hospitalized and recovering.

My then 16-year-old daughter was charged with caring for her younger 1-year-old sibling.

My family stayed at my bedside caring for me.

A Game Changer

Have you ever played the game, hopscotch? It is a childhood game that for many of you may bring back fond childhood memories of jumping from one numbered block to the next.

It did for me, but now the game reminds me of my life.

With a snap of a finger hopscotch was my life's reality.

But instead of advancing to laughter and fun, my life moved from one problem to the next. And none of it was fun.

Surviving and Thriving

My life skipped from one complication to the next. I became mentally and physically exhausted. I wanted to give in to the temptation to quit.

However, I heard the pleading of my mother's prayers, the cry of my father's heart and saw the sadness in my sister's eyes – all willing me to not only survive, but to thrive.

Thankfully, I wasn't a person who gave up easily anyway. So, with a *resiliency* that had become familiar to me, I endured test after test, surgery after surgery.

Chapter Two: Dates to Remember

*"Keep your head up,
God gives his hardest battles to his strongest soldiers."*
-Unknown

During those 54 days so much happened. Some things I was told by my family, but there were other things that will never be erased from my memory. These events are like living journal entries:

July 20, 2019

Today, I am scheduled for a tubal ligation. I was certain it would be a quick and simple process followed by an immediate release from the hospital. I was ready to get home and enjoy my baby girl with the rest of my family. However, that didn't happen. Afterwards, what was immediate was the pain – it was intense and uncontrolled. I became hypotensive (*low blood pressure*), mildly hypoxic (*irritable, poor eating*) and experienced tachycardic (*a fast heart rate*).

July 22, 2019

It has been two days now and I still have no relief. After an x-ray the diagnosis was significant atelectasis (a *complete or partial collapsed lung*)!

July 23, 2019

I thought dealing with a collapsed lung was the worst of things, but after continued pain in my abdomen, they placed a NG tube leading to my abdomen for gastric decomposition. And a feeding tube in my nostrils for nutrition since I refuse to eat. I'm in unbearable pain, very uncomfortable, and due to the NG Tube, I can't speak.

July 26, 2019

Exactly six days after surgery, I began to complain that I was hot. I could see the worry in my family because to them the room was extremely cold! My dad positioned me directly beside the air vent but still wasn't able to cool off. I felt a deep burning inside. It felt like a match had been lit inside of me and the heat was spreading like a wildfire suffocating my bones and my organs.

The Verge of Death

Everyone was puzzled, except my sister. With her medical knowledge she recommended that the doctors look into the possibility of an infection. They agreed but said they would wait until the next day to investigate her theory.

Honestly, I was losing faith and didn't believe I could make it that long.

"I don't think I'm going to make it, Mommie," I said weakly.

"Not on my watch," Mommie said with an attitude.

My momma was my advocate.

"No," she said to the physician. "Shawnise needs to be checked tonight." She was firm, strong, and thankfully they listened.

A CT scan of my abdomen and pelvis was ordered right away and showed a large amount of fecal material in my right colon, colonic ileus (intestinal obstruction), along with intraperitoneal free air, which indicated a perforation (or tear). A General Surgeon was consulted, and I went into emergency, exploratory surgery that same night.

August 16, 2019

It's my birthday! August 16, 2019. By the grace of God, I made it to see my 34th birthday. Instead of a party and cake surrounded by family and friends, I was in CCU diagnosed with acute Hypoxic Respiratory Failure, Acute Renal Failure and Congestive Heart Failure with an ejection fraction of 10-15% blood pumping to my heart. When I finally made it to my private room, I realized I was anemic – I had a scary episode of nose bleeds (*epistaxis*).

August 28th, 2019

I'm going to be discharged tomorrow! I'm so ready to go home. I miss my baby and my daughters. I'm praying my baby girl hasn't forgotten me.

STAT

"Hey sis," my sister said as she entered the room.

"Hey sis," I said back. "How was work?"

"It was a typical day," she said.

As a hospice aid and future LPN, my sister and my mother (a hardworking housekeeper), I was well taken care of and given lots of love and support.

My sister and I laughed, watched TV, and sang praise and worship songs. I was overjoyed with excitement at the prospect of going home the next day.

"Well, I'm going home to get some rest now, sis," she said as she prepared to leave. "See you later."

"Ok love," I said back in high spirits. "Thank you for coming by."

"No problem baby sis," she laughed. "I'll be by first thing in the morning to pick you up. I love you."

"I love you too," I said. I already missed her company.

I went back to being restless as I watched a clock that didn't seem to move.

That state of stillness quickly went away.

The nursing team and head doctor were notified by the heart monitoring department about my abnormal heart reading. The nurse entered the room first. About the time the head doctor arrived a few minutes later I was able to respond to the nurse's questions and my heart reading was stable.

Everyone left the room.

Fifteen minutes later, the heart monitor did its job and reported a reading: CODE BLUE.

A short way to say, URGENT.

I had taken a turn for the worse. The team of doctors and nurses entered my room with a frightening sense of urgency.

"I just left her fifteen minutes ago," I heard one of the doctors say.

Then I heard someone yell, "STAT."

When they entered my room, I was conscious.

"How are you feeling," a doctor asked me.

Before I could respond my heart stopped and I went into ventricular cardiac arrest.

From some place that felt far away, their conversation continued.

'Code Blue!" Someone repeated.

"Oh my god," Another person yelled. "She just had her baby."

August 29th
(and later September 3rd, 2019)

I've had another blood transfusions, but I don't feel any better. Chest x-rays showed I have double pneumonia (*bilateral pulmonary infiltrates versus edema*).

Gosh, is THIS how it ends for me? I wondered.

The multiple antibiotics and BiPAP supported me with breathing and helped me to find strength to walk little by little but with assistance.

Every hour nurses came in to reposition me in an effort to reverse the pneumonia as well as to take the pressure off the bed sores and back pain I had developed.

Unforgettable

I am probably overmedicated but I won't complain. I was given many medicines to ease my pain and suffering. Morphine, Oxycodone, and Percocet felt like savers especially when it was time to change the Wound VAC dressing on my abdomen.

Being able to look deep into my open abdomen and the smell of my flesh are two things I will never forget.

It has been three days and the double pneumonia has subsided.

Wont He do it?!

Dates to Remember Photos

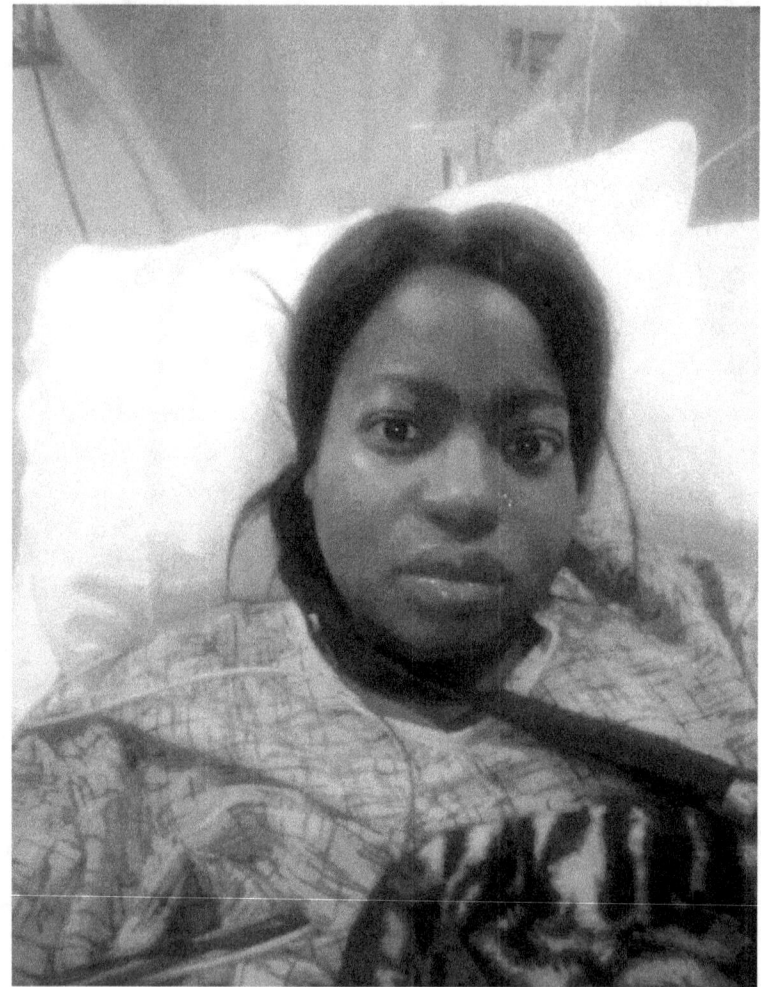

Photo 3 "Did this really happen?

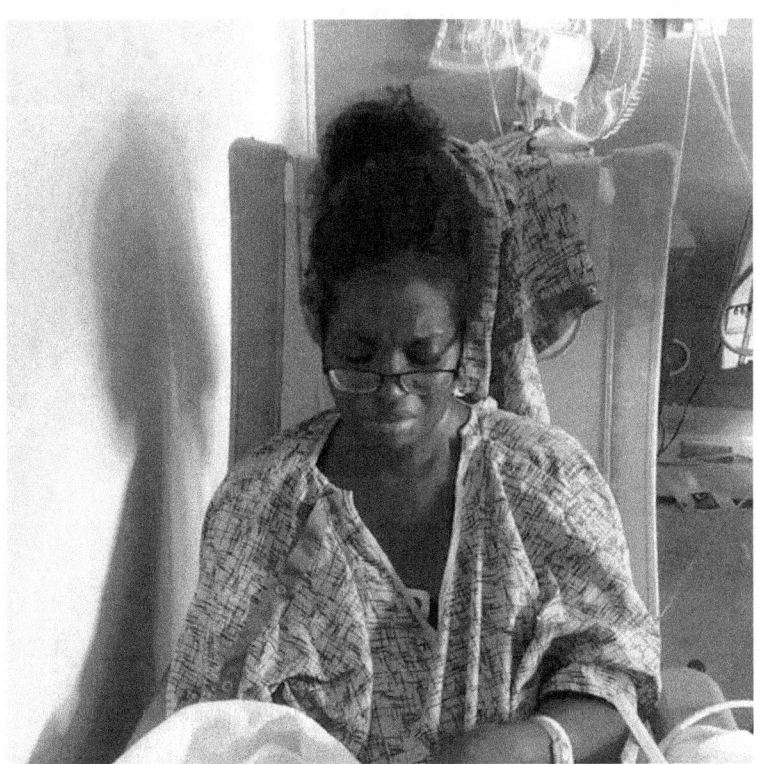

Photo 4 "The pain was unbearable."

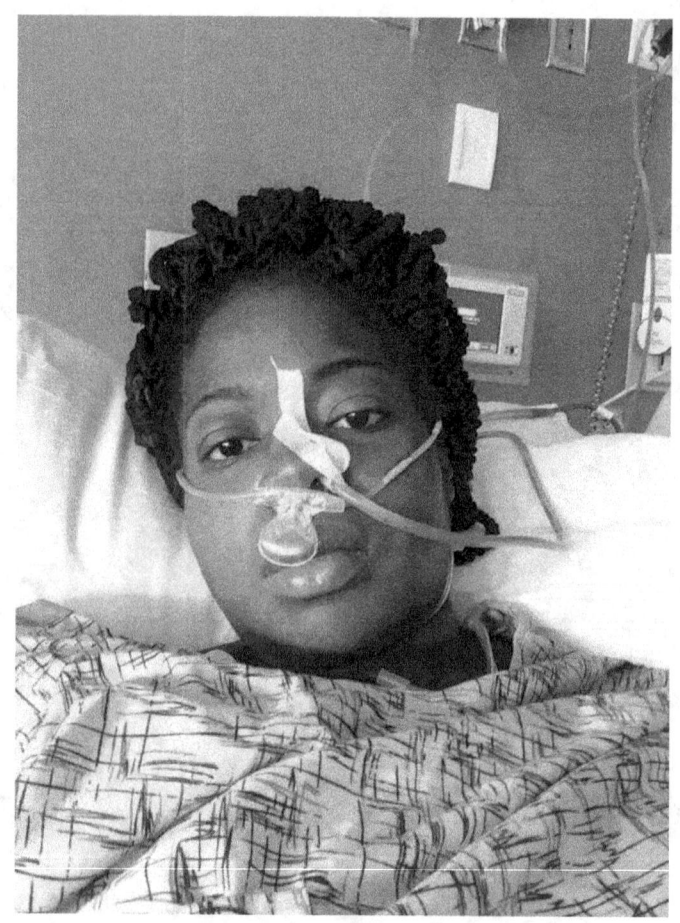
Photo 5 "I knew God had a plan."

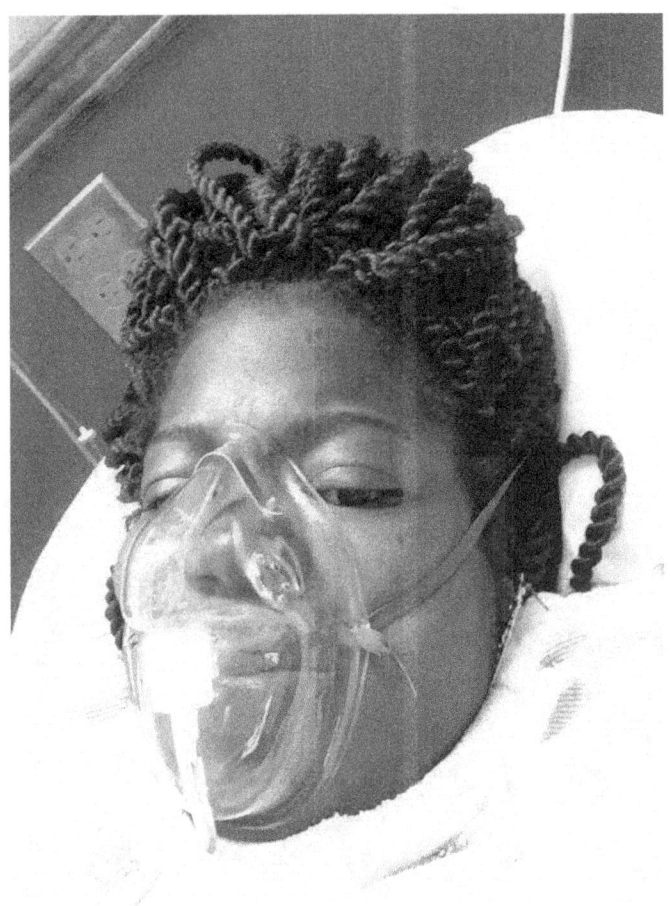

Photo 6 "I'm so qrateful my family was there."

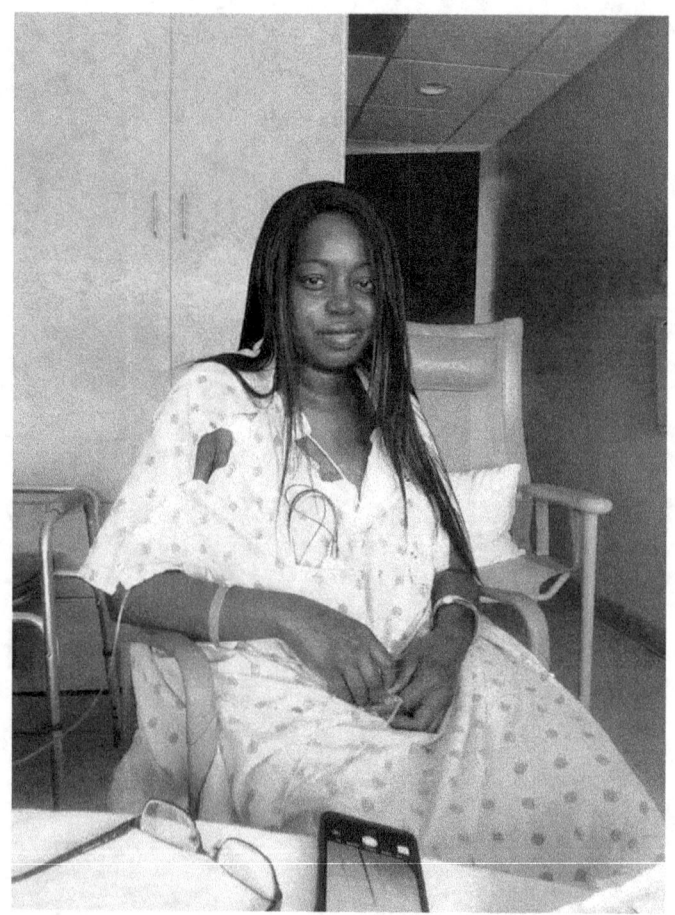
Photo 7 "Getting back my strength was essential."

Chapter Three: Spiritual Ascension

*"Even when I walk through the darkest valley,
I will not be afraid, for you are close beside me..."*
Psalm 23:4 (NLT)

There are some things that we are taught about life, death, and even Heaven that may be off the mark. Prior to my experience, I had long held beliefs that don't reconcile to what I know now.

I Didn't Mean To Die

Before I could answer the doctor's question as to how I was doing, I felt my spirit instantaneously leave my body.

I felt myself leaving behind the weight of my physical body.

Only moments before, I heard, "Code blue," and witnessed the fury of activity around me as they attempted to save my life.

I had no sense of pain, and I didn't feel the breaking of my ribs as the lucas device was administering CPR. I also didn't feel the five electrical shocks to my heart.

What I did feel was an enormous sense of peace.

I had an awareness:

My body is there, I thought. *but I am here.*

I had the knowledge that I was in a place separate from my physical body. Along with that awareness came a complete shock and fear. I had an appointment with death. I just couldn't reschedule, miss, or cancel. It was my time – an appointment for me and me only.

It all happened so fast with ease. It was as though death came like a thief in the night.

Oh no, I thought. *I just died. I didn't mean to die!*

The Light

Swiftly, a calmness came over me like a soft and comfortable blanket. I felt reassured that I was going to be ok. I felt like I had just gained some sort of superpower. I was immortal floating towards a warm and inviting being of light from a dark tunnel. I felt pure and light as a feather floating up effortlessly towards that light.

The light was mesmerizing. I couldn't take my eyes off it, and I was deeply engaged.

The dark tunnel turned into rays of vibrant light, a blend of futuristic colors and the space that was around me and beyond me was endless. There was no need to turn around to look behind me because everything was in my peripheral vision.

Then, I heard the most beautiful musical sounds I'd ever heard. And I continued to be mesmerized.

Peace That Surpasses Understanding

The peace was indescribable.

I was being called closer to the light and the closer I got, the deeper peace I felt.

I felt special, angelic, connected, welcomed, home, loved, and a wholeness. I felt smiled upon and forgiveness. I wasn't worried, stressed, hungry, thirsty or in pain.

There was no notion of time.

Somehow, I knew I was on my way to meet God and I was comfortable. I was able to see and hear the flow of prayers! It's as if the prayers were objects and I was passing them by. It felt as if I was receiving gifts!

Awe, all of this for me? I thought with a big smile.

I know one thing for sure – GOD HEARS PRAYERS!

I can't say with certainty who was praying, but I saw them. I know our prayers reach heaven. And I had a sense that each of the prayers I felt were for me!

They were GRAND prayers.

It is for this reason that I now feel the more prayers we pray, the merrier – especially when it comes to praying for someone else.

I also knew that someone close to me was pleading on my behalf in the presence of GOD.

If I had to guess, I think it was the spirit of my grandfather who I adored and had missed so much.

God With Me In The Valley

"This means that anyone who belongs to Christ has become a new person. The old life is gone; a new life has begun."
2 Corinthians 5:17 NLT

As I eased into a garden there was one particular flower that intrigued me. It was a burgundy – reddish colored Lily. It stood out among all the other flowers. The stem of the flower was translucent, and you could see the flow of life and energy!

This was my glimpse into paradise. This was my rebirth, a butterfly effect.

This experience was higher than my human mind could phantom, so what happened afterward is a blur to my memory.

I am not sure if I had a choice to stay or return.

There was a part of me that wanted to stay but there was another side that wanted to return to my babies and family.

On my own, I knew I couldn't turn around. But somehow, I did, and it felt like time travel backwards as I transported back into my physical body. It was like being sucked through a portal.

God was with me.

Chapter Four: Craziness

"You never know how strong you are until being strong is the only choice you have"
-Bob Marley

As I was dealing with this life and death situation – the craziness of being revived, chaos was also erupting for my family.

Coding

"You need to get back to the hospital," a frantic nurse was telling my sister over the phone, as she was approaching her home. This was the type of call no loved one wants to receive.

"Why," she asked matching the nurse's tone. "What is it?"

"Ms. Chantell is in distress," the nurse said. "Please contact her parents as well."

Unsure of what was happening or what to expect upon her arrival, my sister hurried back to the hospital.

"What's going on?" She shouted at the doctors as she entered my room.

Because she was still in her scrubs, they assumed she was employed with the hospital.

"What do you mean what is going on?" The doctor shouted back. "She coded."

Looking around the room, my sister took in all the equipment, people, and activity. But when she saw what had already happened, my lifeless eyes popped out my eye sockets, she fainted.

That is when they realized she was not staff, but a family member. Someone helped her on her feet and rushed her out of the room while the rest of the medical staff continued to work tirelessly for the next twenty minutes to revive me.

Eventually, my parents were notified. Everyone gathered in a private room close by and remained there until they were notified that I was stabilized.

A Miraculous Recovery

In order to reduce the pressure from my brain and heart, I was placed in a medically induced coma.

For 48 hours, I was intubated and then weaned from the ventilator. While on the ventilator, I could hear the voice of my mother saying, "You can beat this Niecy." As she softly brushed her hand across my forehead, she continued to whisper words of comfort and calling me by my childhood nickname:

"Niecy, open your eyes baby."

My mother's voice was my indication that I was near her and still alive.

While my improvement was very slow, it was clear to everyone around me that it was miraculous.

I wasn't a vegetable!

Before I woke up, they weren't sure how much damage had been done because I'd gone without oxygen for a while.

"What happened?" I asked as I looked into the worried faces of my family.

"Sweetheart," my mom began, "your heart stopped beating for twenty minutes."

"What?" I said in obvious disbelief. I looked at my sister and continued to ask, "What happened Tia?"

As my family told me all that happened to me, I sat in quiet disbelief. They said they realized there had been some kind of brain injury because I kept asking them the same questions over and over.

Why? I wondered. *What was the purpose for taking me and then allowing me to come back?*

Homegoing

Finally, on September 11, 2019, I was discharged to go home. I was excited but also very nervous.

Instead of going home with my baby, I went home with ejection fraction of 25-30% blood pumping to my heart. This indicated that my heart muscle was still weak and that I was still in the range of heart failure.

I had been prescribed more than 20 pills to take every day, a life vest, an IV Milrinone in my arm (for cardiac support), a picc line in my chest, and a wound VAC.

It was a lot and just when I thought I was on the road to recovery, I was readmitted to another hospital the very next day as I was showing signs of a stoke!

Three days later I was discharged but less than 48 hours later, my dad gets a call that the lab showed E.coli and for me to be readmitted for treatment.

I cried and cried. I did not want to return to the hospital. Thankfully a different doctor called us before we left for the hospital. She told us the E.coli was the type that could be treated from home.

If someone had told me that I could not only endure all of this, but survive it, I would not have believed them.

I believe God gives us the strength we need to do whatever He has purposed for us to do.

Photo Gallery

Photo 8 Author and Mom

Photo 9 Author and Dad

Photo 10 Author and Sister

Photo 11 Author - My rebirth

Photo 12 Author - My rebirth

Photo 13 Author - My rebirth

Photo 14 Author - My rebirth

Photo 15 Author and all three of her children.

Photo 16 Baby Kensi and Auntie Rita (RIP Auntie)

Photo 17 Author, baby Naomi, and Grandma

Chapter Five: Remembrance

*"For everything there is a season,
and a time for every purpose under heaven…"*
Ecclesiastes 3:1

Turns out the reason I couldn't remember things right away was because apparently, they gave me medications to wipe out the memory of the trauma.

And although some things are still vague, the memories did come back.

I believe God allowed me to keep the memories that were important. I'll always cherish the memories of my near-death experience. And I know he allowed me to have them so that I could share them with the world.

Near-Death

It wasn't until several months later that I had remembrance of my out-of-body, near-death experience. I hadn't even known that the term near-death experience even existed.

My memory returned with a clinical diagnosis – Post Traumatic Stress Disorder (PTSD).

Overcoming

And while I overcame some things like the effects of a stroke (drooling of the mouth, tremors of upper and lower extremities while conscious, slurred speech, difficulty swallowing and walking) I am terrified of hospitals, needles, and operating rooms.

Thankfully my bowels responded to treatment and began to function normally, but what remained was a loss of memory and independence.

Life became terrifying. I was depressed. I'd lost my sense of pleasure and felt powerless and anxious. I didn't have a job and didn't know where my next meal would come from.

I was afraid to go to sleep and due to the many medications, I experienced hair loss.

I think there are things worse than death.

Moments

Now more than ever, I have come to know that life is just a series of moments. The spirit doesn't' belong here; it is just passing through.

I let go of temporary things and although I have days where I'm up – there are other days I'm down, I'm able to see the light that exists in this world. While it isn't as bright as the light that awaits us in heaven, it does exist.

In spite of all that was going on, I graduated from Cardiac Rehab 2020 from The Heart Hospital (where I previously worked) and changed my daily diet. This gave me a sense of accomplishment. My recovery is followed by a Heart Transplant Specialist and electrophysiologist who monitor my heart electrical activities and arrhythmia.

Seasons

Just as the bible says, for everything there is a season.

Most days I feel inspired by my Near Death and Out-of-body experience. It's very hard to adjust, once you get to know or meet your inner spirit outside your physical body. It's been two years and I am still trying to process it.

Congestive heart failure doesn't define me and I want to spend each moment with my children and inspire others. August 16, 2021, marks my 36th birthday. I have a lot to be thankful for. I am a survivor; I am a Miracle, and I am Loved. If I had one message to share, it would be that LOVE is the KEY to Eternity!

And God holds the KEY to tomorrow!

Chapter Six: God's Blessings

*"Your illness does not define you;
your strength and courage does."*

-Unknown

The birth of my youngest daughter began a series of events that nearly took my life. Even still, I wouldn't trade being a mother for nothing in this world.

Alexis

I became a mom for the first time in 2003. Alexis was glued to my side for the entire 3-4 days I was in the hospital. After her delivery, I refused to let Alexis out of my sight – not even for a second!

I was only 17 so my emotions ranged from fear to excitement but overwhelmingly, I knew this life-changing journey I was on would provide me with the drive I needed to meet the responsibility to take care of this remarkable, healthy being created by God.

Here was someone more important than me.

Alexis taught me patience, joy after pains, selflessness, and unconditional love. She had a pureness in her beauty. She was a good, quiet baby - so loving.

I cherished each milestone moment in her life. She helped evolve me into the mother I am today.

Her name, which means little helper, is so appropriate. She was always my *lil* helper.

Relying on my upbringing of hard work and perseverance, I worked a full-time job while completing my senior year of high school.

I didn't have an option. I had to keep my baby warm, safe, and cared for.

I was child who had a child, and so Alexis and I practically grew up together. She's not only my daughter, but she's also my best friend.

With Alexis, I realized my choices were lessons that came with an opportunity to not only know better but to do better. I was determined to be the mother God had destined me to be.

As the seasoned folks would say, "It's time to put on your big girl panties and walk in big shoes."

We made it this far by God's grace!

Naomi Grace

In 2019 at the age 32, I welcomed Naomi Grace into our family. She weighed in perfectly at 8lbs, 3 oz, and 19 1/2 inches long.

Her beauty was mesmerizing!

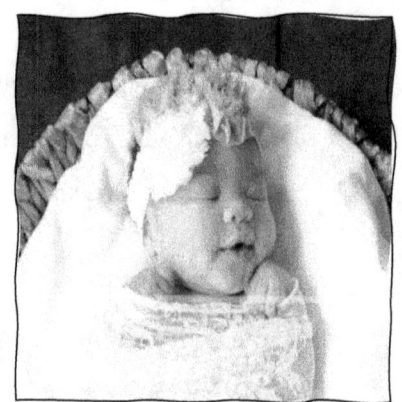

My baby and I shared a unique and immediate bond.

The name Naomi is from the Book of Ruth in the bible and was given to me by the voice of God during my first trimester.

The song "Your grace and mercy" sung by the Mississippi Mass Choir always resonated with me as a child so, "Grace" was chosen as her middle name.

The story of Naomi's life in the bible illustrates the power of God to bring something good out of bitter circumstances.

God Within the Lily

At the time God whispered this name to me, I had no idea why. Now, I realize it represents strength, beauty, and pleasantness – all of which is a nod to my daughter Naomi's character.

The name is special, merciful, and graceful.

God knew I needed Naomi Grace in my heart in order to get through the storm that was to come.

Kensi

One month before baby Naomi's first birthday, I was admitted to the hospital where I gave birth to Naomi's little sister, Kensi Elise.

Kensi was the last child I bore and the first for her father. Although the delivery was without complications, due to the complications from the tubal ligation, I missed out on those first moments of bonding with my baby.

We didn't get the skin-to-skin interaction or breast feeding. In spite of this, Kensi definitely has my sassy yet humble and sweet personality.

As much as I wanted to keep baby Kensi close to me, I had to send her to live with her dad.

That day was a very depressing day.

I longed for the day when I would be reunited with Kensi so that I could love and nurture her during the early stages of her life as I'd done for my other babies.

I had been on my own during the pregnancy and the likelihood of caring for Kensi full-time now with all that was happening to me was unlikely.

I cried with a sense of helplessness and guilt over being too sick to care for Kensi. I blamed myself for what was happening. After all, it had been my choice to have a tubal ligation.

I was heartbroken and felt as if my child had been stolen – ripped from my arms.

The frequent visits with her helped me. I needed to see that my baby was healthy, beautiful, and being cared for. It made life worth living.

Chapter Seven: Faith and Family

"Truly I tell you, if you have faith as small as a mustard seed, you can say to this mountain, 'Move from here to there,' and it will move."
Matthew 17:20

My choice to have a tubal ligation began a series of health problems. My faith was seriously tested.

After each surgery, procedure, or new medicine I expected to get better, but I only got worse.

Each floor of the hospital specialized in a different care, and it seems I spent time on each of them at one point or another.

Mustard Seed Faith

"Let not your heart be troubled; ye believe in God, believe in me."
John 14:1-3

From day to day, it was no telling where you'd find me!

I was in and out of the CCU and then finally placed on the heart failure floor.

I talked to God and declared healing.

I knew He was a Way maker and that he had and would continue to bring me through life's trials.

On my death bed, I spoke to God:

God,
You said that all I needed was the faith of a small mustard seed. Lord, I have been faithful and now it is time for You to deliver me. I want out. I want to go home to be with my family.

Like Naomi in the bible, I felt forgotten by God.

I began to ask for understanding.

Why this Lord? Why me?

I didn't know that I was being prepared for something BIG, something GREAT!

God took me from my physical body in that hospital bed and brought me closer to Him to show me how much He love me – how much He loves his children.

God showed me a glimpse of the home He has prepared for me in eternity. In the earthly time of twenty minutes, I was clinically dead, and it was magical.

My spirit was filled and felt accepted.

God showed me what mustard seed size faith can do.

And on September 11, 2019, I was discharged to go home.

Power of Family

My family took turns assisting in Naomi's care. I too was blessed to have around the clock visits from family and friends.

While in the hospital for nearly 2 1/2 months there wasn't a day that I didn't see either my mom, dad, sister, Auntie Brenda, Auntie Ellamae or Cousin Steven.

My mom and sister worked and so they visited before or after work and on their days off. My dad stayed overnight with me frequently.

When I needed my family the most, they were there for me.

They communicated about my care to each other and knew what to ask the doctors. When the doctor made his rounds around 4:30 am my mom was right there.

I saw at least 7-10 doctors each day.

My sister knew more about the medical aspect of things because of her medical background.

My dad had the hospital administrator on speed dial.

All of my needs were cared for because I was fortunate to have a family that was present and involved.

My bed stayed neat and clean. My family ensured that I wasn't dirty and that my environment was clean.

Hospital baths in my condition consisted of cold baby wipes. Every so often I was able to get a warm bed bath, but I always felt less clean without a shower.

My sister changed the game when she gave me the best bed bath of my life. She was thorough and patient when washing me.

One time when I was able to shower for the first time, she washed my hair and gave me the best shower. Her comforting care gave me hope and I felt loved.

The Hospice patients that she works with daily really has the hands and heart of an angel caring for them.

Dignity? What's That?

When I was in an incontinence condition, I had a catheter then gradually went into adult diapers and the use of a white wick which is basically an external catheter which catches and absorbs the urine to aid in less frequent trips to the potty.

My dignity was next to the last thing that went before I died. Due to my bowels failing to work properly I began to grossly vomit my bowels out of my mouth repeatedly.

Being able to form a bowel and increasing my strength to raise myself off the toilet seat was such a momentous feat!

It is the little things that were bringing about the greatest praise.

I thanked God for each day.

I had no strength to wipe myself and my mom gave me her strength. My mom is the most kindhearted person I have ever known.

Being stubborn and admittedly too proud, I decided to pull myself out of bed unattended. I walked slowly towards the potty. I was so weak that I fell through the eating table next to the potty, hitting my head hard on the hospital floor.

I guess the noise I made caught the attention of the nurses and they rushed in to assist me.

The loud crash woke up my dad. Finding me on the floor left him furious.

Me and my dignity stayed in bed for days after that.

God Within the Lily

Chapter Eight: My Altered Life

"Perhaps you were born for such a time like this."
Esther 4:14

My taste for food declined and I was unable to hold it down anyway, so I stopped eating.

There was also a fear that if I ate my bowels wouldn't form and back up and out of my mouth!

While I'd been in the hospital, I'd missed out on a lot of family functions. Our family is large and close knit; we love seeing each other.

Mind vs Body

My dad did all he could to make life seem normal for me while I was in the hospital. The simplest things became challenging.

I wasn't able to eat the plate of barbecue, but the smell of it gave me life!

At my request, my mom would bring me other foods hoping that I'd eat. But when I got it, I had no appetite for it.

In my mind I wanted those foods badly, but my body couldn't accept it. Mentally I was scared to eat.

Even with the strict diet later, I choose liquids. Eventually I graduated to puree foods because I was unable to use my throat muscles for swallowing.

Advocates and Friends

Respiratory therapy and physical therapy became a daily regimen. The simplest tasks were the most difficult, but I didn't give up trying.

In my mind I was doing it and trying to get better for my babies.

Three or four days a week, I had wound vac dressing replaced.

I will never forget the very first time I saw them clean the wound and replace the vac.

My mom was present, to observe the process. When I saw the shock in her eyes at my incision, I looked at my abdomen. I saw the inside of my stomach and it was gross. The smell was horrible!

As the tech began to pull back the tape, I reacted.

"Oooouch," I hollered. Then screamed as loud as I could. They may as well have been pulling duct tape from an open burn wound.

I was blessed to have my mom there.

While holding my hand, my mother addressed the tech in a firm tone:

"She needs to have something for the pain!" She told him. "She is never to have this procedure again without something to help with the pain."

The tech did not consider the enormous pain I would feel when the tape was pulled back.

My mom held my hand and was very firm in letting the techs know to never undress my wound without giving me something!

From that point on, morphine became my friend. (Although my family told me that the morphine had me talking out of my head.)

Effects of Electrical shock

After the cardiac arrest, my face and skin lacked proper blood flow. My lips were extremely black, sore and dry.

I had no control over my drooling, so I went through towel after towel and many mouth sponges.

Brain injury and side effects to the meds caused me to have tremors. Holding a cup of water seemed impossible.

I was told and given heat packs to alternate with cold packs to ease the soreness of my chest. The shock pedals were at such high voltage I could see the imprint that it left.

My skin was fried and with every lifting of the hot or cold pack a piece of my skin came with it.

The CPR administer from the lucas device cracked my ribs.

There was a lot that went into saving my life and there was even more that went with living after dying.

With time, proper rest and air supply, I was able to heal.

I've heard so many people say that God doesn't put more on us than we can bear. I am living witness to that truth.

God Within the Lily

Chapter Nine: Recovery

When you experience trauma, not only are certain memories ingrained but there are certain people for whom you will never forget.

There was one nurse I connected with who took the time out of her busy day to wheel me outside so I could feel the sunlight because it had been more than a month since I'd been outdoors!

Prior to this experience, I'd never spent more than a few days inside a hospital. And those times had been happy – giving birth to my daughters.

Needless to say, being hospitalized for 54 days was a huge challenge.

Motherly Comfort

One night while in ICU I was having an anxiety attack. My breathing was laboring for over 40 minutes. It was frustrating and scary as I was unable to catch my breath.

"Breathe slowly," the nurse repeated sternly. "In your mouth and out your nose."

Maybe she wasn't aware that I'd never had an anxiety attack before. I didn't need her to be mean. I needed assistance with breathing.

"I want my momma," I managed to say as I cried.

It was late and mom wasn't there.

After nearly an hour of agony, God sent an Angel to the rescue!

Nurse Practitioner Allen came into my room. I wasn't even her patient at the time.

"Shawnise," she said in the sweetest, motherly tone. "It is going to be ok. I'm here for you. You are not alone."

She never knew I recognized her from my job at the Arkansas heart hospital clinic. Her familiar face made all the difference in the world.

I passed out and was given Ativan and woke up with a nice cool breeze from the BIPAP. After that, I found myself relying heavily on the BIPAP. I was scared that without it, I'd have another anxiety attack. I was afraid to rely on my own lungs for breathing.

Eventually, I learned to trust the process and worked hard with my breathing exercises.

Road to Recovery

I had been looking forward to going home for so long but I never stopped to consider how challenging it would be.

My thoughts were of my family, good food, and my comfortable bed!

However, when I arrived home things were so different. I had been without my comfy bed for so long it was hard to relax in it.

Everywhere I sat in my home felt like a torturous hard hospital bed. My dad retrieved a leather recliner from the side of road. Someone considered it trash, but for me it was a treasure. We sanitized it and that is where I spent most of my days with my feet elevated trying to control fluid retention.

As for good food, I was only capable of eating mash potatoes, eggs, apple sauce, and whatever was super soft.

A home health nurse was provided to me to help me manage my medication, doctor appointments, wound dressing.

The home health nurse also managed my IV medicine, life vest, wound vac.

She trained my dad and I on how to read the devices and replace the batteries.

On a weekly basis I had medical supplies and IV medications delivered at my doorstep. She went above and beyond the call of duty by getting my life saving medications down from $300 and $400 dollars to zero!

Prior to my home health nurse arriving to administer the milirone drip to my arm, my dad and I had to remember to remove the IV bag from the refrigerator. This had to be done at least two hours before she arrived for safety reasons.

God Within the Lily

Chapter Ten: God's Provisions

Little by little I was gaining my independence back. I remember having to take really quick showers because I had to wear the life vest 24/7.

I carefully learned how to connect the leads to a clean life vest. There were times that I had to wrap my arm in saran wrap to keep the IV dry while I bathe or showered. I developed a small routine so I could do more stuff on my own.

Patience

Patience was not my virtue. I was so tired of feeling worthless. I decided to drive my car one day. My family didn't think I was ready, and they were right, but I had to get out of the house and find some form of normalcy.

While I was on my way home - 15 minutes away, my IV Medicine bag began to beep, indicating the battery was low and the machine would turn off.

This was a matter of life and death; so I drove way over the speed limit to get home to replace the battery.

As luck would have it, a cop pulled me over.

"Ma'am, I need to see your license and registration."

"I'm sorry officer," I said in a hurry. "But my IV is beeping and if I don't get home in time to change the battery, I could die!"

He looked at me skeptically at first. But when I held up my arm for him to see the cord and he heard the beeping, realization sank in.

"Ok ma'am," he said waving me away. "Go on but please slow down. You won't make it in time if you have an accident."

Taking his advice, I slowed down but drove towards home with purpose and determination.

I made it home in the nick of time and needless to say I learned a valuable lesson.

Trust God and my family.

My body needed time to heal.

Life vest malfunctioned

One day my dad and I left the house to run errands. When we returned, Dad helped me out of the car and as I was walking with my walker towards my front door I felt a burning sensation. As I continued to walk, the sensation got stronger and stronger.

I grimaced loudly.

"Whats the matter Shawnise," Dad asked instantly worried.

"My back feels like it is on fire," I said now in agony.

We ripped the life vest off and saw a lot of blue gushy stuff on the life vest. It was also all over my back.

Apparently, the life vest had exploded!

The wires had come in contact with the liquid and that is what was burning my back.

It was one thing after another.

Cardiac Rehab

Not all parts of my recovery were bad. There were some things I looked forward to.

Cardiac rehab was something I enjoyed. My momma was my plus one to work out with me. We were able to see live cooking shows that demonstrated better cooking habits.

We also did yoga workouts too. I loved spending time with my mom.

Cardiac rehab helped me to understand my condition and the outcome of healthy eating and daily workout.

Finances

> *"And my God will supply every need of yours according to his riches in glory in Christ Jesus."*
> *Philippians 4:19*

I didn't work for months but God still provided.

Not one of my utilities or services was turned off. Mailbox blessings kept my bills paid and six months later I was approved for social security.

I am legally blind and was blessed with a six months' supply of contacts from a great friend. This was just one less thing to worry about.

God is my source for everything!

He supplies all my needs, and I won't deny Him.

A New Shawnise

"After your season of suffering God in all his Grace will restore, confirm, strengthen, and establish you."
Peter 5:10

Two years after my ordeal, my heart is pumping blood at 40 percent, and I have 80 % battery life left on the defibrillator.

My life now consists of heart medicines, a lot of natural products, herbs, and home remedies. I am certainly a healthier me.

The first couple of months at home were very rough. I was trying to heal and be a parent.

I felt overwhelmed.

Carrying a newborn while wearing a life vest and an IV in my arm and wound vac connected to my abdomen was a lot of weight to carry – physically and emotionally.

I've heard it said that to whom much is given, much is required.

Sometimes I feel like a stranger in this body because my spirit was disconnected from it.

I believe the day of the cardiac arrest the old Shawnise died.

This new Shawnise had *much* happen to her. And now, I am determined to give back *much* in return.

> "But I am confident that neither death nor life nor angels, nor principalities, nor things present, nor things to come, nor power, nor height, nor depth, nor any other creative thing will be able to separate us from the love of God which is in Christ Jesus our Lord."
> Romans 8:38-39

God Within the Lily

Conclusion: Here's What Happened

After the tubal ligation, exploratory surgery was performed to determine the cause of my discomfort.

Once my abdomen was opened, the surgeon noticed a return of free air and a large amount of juice (succus) - a little over 3.5 liters. She also noticed that my bowels were in poor condition with a fair amount of fluid (exudate) present.

Further exploring my abdomen, she discovered a recent 0.5 cm bowel injury and several interloop abscesses.

The surgeon was able to remove the abscesses and rinse out my intestine thoroughly checking for additional punctures.

After surgery, a wound VAC was placed over the incision along with two drain tubes inserted due to high risks of infection.

The left drain was placed in my pelvic area behind my enlarged uterus and the right drain was placed within my small bowel.

I was sent to PACU (Post-Anesthesia Care Unit) for close observation after surgery and treatment.

Cultures revealed I had three life threatening infections (Klebsiella oxytoca, streptococcus anginosus and enterococcus hirae).

Unfortunately, these infections had gone untreated for days and had entered my bloodstream and were attacking my organs.

I became septic. The smell and taste of bowel coming out my mouth was toxic!

After 54 days in the hospital, I was discharged home only to be readmitted to a different hospital the very next day with concerns of a stroke (CVA).

Over the course of several days, I was treated for acutely worsening stuttering (aphasia). Basically, I was experiencing stroke-like symptoms.

An MRI showed volume loss in my brain.

I also had a swallowing test and at the time I was only able to eat pureed foods.

After I was discharged from there, I tested positive for E Coli which thankfully I could be treated for it from home.

December 4, 2019 I had to go in for a S-ICD placement (also known as a defibrillator).

In 2019 I saw the operation room more than six times for the following:

-Tubal Ligation
-Exploratory Laparotomy to Repair small bowel injury
-Drainage of intraabdominal abscess/drainage placement x 2
-Wound Vac placement to incision
-Abscessogram x 4, EGD,
-Picc line placement had I had undergone multiple drain placements in my pelvic, and ICD

> *"I can do all things through Christ that strengthens me." Philippians."*
> *4:13*

My sickness and death not only affected me, but it affected the people connected to me – including my children. Everyone was exhausted, stressed, overwhelmed, and grieving over my situation in their own way.

Trouble don't last always.

I knew I had to push and press my way through in order to relieve the burden my health had caused everyone.

In fact, others have questioned my fitness as a mother. I had to prove that by any means my kids were in good hands.

The real VIPs in all of this are my family. They stood by me with these babies every step of the way.

In many ways, I'm stronger, better, and a much healthier mom. My illness does not define me because I have the strength, courage, and mindset to overcome the odds.

God Within the Lily

About the Author

Arkansas native, Shawnise Chantell, was born in 1985 from the union of her father, Willie Powell and mother, Kathy Stewart. The mother of three amazing daughters appreciates her upbringing.

Staying true to her lioness personality traits and cultural essence has always propelled Shawnise to be a warrior, work hard, and persevere through life's challenges and crisis. Shawnise has always had a big heart and is naturally gifted to service and care for others. After witnessing her mother's younger sibling dying at age sixteen from terminal cancer, she felt called to care for others which led to a thriving career in healthcare.

After High School Shawnise went to Pulaski Technical College where she exceled in her studies (making the Dean's List) and socially by pledging Phi Theta Kappa Beta Zeta Omega Chapter. Shawnise earned a certificate of completion in Medical Transcription in May 2007 and later graduated from The University of Arkansas for Medical Science with an Associates of Applied Science in Health Information Technology in December 2014.

At the Arkansas Heart Hospital, Shawnise had the great privilege of working with cardiologist, Dr. Riberio for three years. She later had the opportunity to work with Dr. Kane, Dr. Nash and the Cardiovascular & Thoracic Surgical Team before her traumatic medical experience and subsequent permanent disability.

One night during her first year of recovery, while watching television, Chantell witnessed chest compression administered to woman who was experiencing a cardiac arrest. The scene was instantly triggering because of the author's own experience.

Visions of the distressful event sparked feelings of grief, anxiety, and depression.

At her father's recommendation, the author sought help from a psychiatrist and counselor to help her process the trauma. The therapy was life-altering and partly what the author credits with her current journey towards recovery. Her decision to seek help has inspired her to turn her trials into triumphs. Her hope is that by sharing her story, *God Within the Lily*, with others she can help others turn their life around as well.

Shawnise enjoys a good read filled with compassion, truth, and medical history. Her favorite book, *The Immortal Life of Henrietta Lacks*, was initially a reading assignment in college but became so much more! In addition to reading, Shawnise is a fan of performance arts. She likes to read poems and paint. Considering herself diverse and adventurous, in her spare time the author loves exploring nature, traveling, and staying active in general. However, moments with her family are what the author cherishes most.

Cain's birthday, August 16, has always grand and celebrated event. However, she now thanks God that she can celebrate a second birthday (or rebirth) on August 28; the day God declared that she would live and not die!

If you were inspired by my story, please leave an Amazon review and pass on what I shared with you to someone else. Everyone can use positive encouragement.

For more information, please contact the author:

The Shawnise Chantell Story

PO Box 5444

Jacksonville AR 72078

Telephone: 612 PURPOSE

612-787-7073

Email: theshawnisechantellstory@gmail.com

Website: www.shawnisechantell.com

Social Media (Twitter, LinkedIn, Facebook & Instagram) @authorshawnisechantell

God Within the Lily

He is BEFORE all things

A Note from the Publisher

"... Touch not mine anointed..."
1 Chronicles 16:22 (KJV)

God **Within the Lily** *is a precious book. In addition to highlighting God's grace, mercy, and plan for our lives, author Shawnise Chantell does an incredible job of relaying the importance of family.*

As I reviewed the manuscript and spoke with the author, the love for life and family was powerful.

Before we even began the editing process, I had a strong urge to speak with Ms. Chantell's family.

I knew how she was affected by what happened to her, but I wanted to know from them (her mom and dad in particular) how their lives were impacted as well.

I've often said that our challenges are not only ours. Anyone who has loved anyone will agree with that.

As a mother, I consider my children and grandchildren extensions of me. It is as if my heart duplicated itself and then grew arms and legs.

What happens to your child – happens to you.

It is true of underage children, but even more so with adult children. And many ways, it feels worse because you are left helpless to watch them as they navigate life.

Just as God is protective over his children, so is a mother/parent.

***

Describe Shawnise before the event:

My daughter is smart, and college educated. She was a go-getter.

She was adventurous. She loved jumping out of parachutes, climbing mountains, and riding bikes. She was the most adventurous person I knew – in the beginning. She enjoyed life!

She was also athletic and enjoyed swimming too. But she also was a hard worker. She went to work every day.

Now she cannot do most of the things she used to do because of the emotional and physical trauma she's experienced.

She wants to do those things she used to do, but she is also afraid because of the resulting medical complications

Now instead of a zest for life, she is afraid of life. This event has left her afraid to live life. She went from being fearless to fearful.

A lot was taken from her.

God Within the Lily

When did you first know that something was wrong?

Her older sister and I work in the healthcare industry. We've both had tubal ligations, so when the procedure took longer than they told us it would, we wondered what was going on. No one came to tell us anything, so we were already worried.

But when we learned she couldn't breastfeed the baby, that is when we knew something wasn't right.

Why couldn't she breastfeed?

Shawnise had plans to breastfeed her baby. She had been very adamant about that. This would be her last baby, and she wanted to experience all the things a new mom could. So, when the nurse came to us asking what to do about feeding the baby – we knew something wasn't right. *Why couldn't Shawnise breastfeed her baby?*

Still unaware of what was happening but hearing the baby crying, we quickly decided to have them go ahead and bottle feed the baby instead.

What did this do for the concerns you already had over the procedure taking so long?

It made me even more concerned. Shawnise was a very healthy person before the birth of her third child. And women have been having babies and tubal ligations for many years. So, this wasn't something new they were trying on an unhealthy, sick person.

So, what went wrong? Why was her situation different? Did something happen to her?

When did you notice a change in Shawnise's demeanor?

Shawnise was very self-sufficient. She didn't like to rely on people or be a burden. If she could do it herself, she wanted to, and she would.

Which is why she nearly hurt herself.

One morning, Shawnise woke up with an urgency to use the bedside toilet. Her dad was asleep on the sofa beside her, but Shawnise didn't want to disturb his sleep. She pressed the call light. There was a long response as usual. Finally, they said they'd be right in but that wasn't the case.

So, Shawnise attempted to go on her own. But she didn't make it. Instead, her strength gave out as she stood up on her feet. She broke through the tray table wrapped with her many cords and hit her head hard on the floor!

The loud commotion woke up her father and he was furious. By the concern of her dad he contacted the head hospital official and they immediately checked out the incident and ordered a MRI on Shawnise's brain to ensure there wasn't bleeding.

Other than not being able to breastfeed her baby, were there other signs that something was seriously wrong?

The room was freezing. It was 60 degrees in that room. The doctors were cold. The nurses were cold. We were all cold, but Shawnise kept complaining that she was hot. Shawnise later told me it was like being set on fire from the inside out by gasoline.

We put a cold, wet towel around her and moved her closer to the AC unit, but she couldn't get cool.

And that's when her sister and I knew what was going on.

In the medical field, we recognize this as infection!

I knew there was an infection, but I didn't know where. So, I told the nurses right away what I suspected and that I wanted someone to do something NOW.

This was my child!

After you told them what you suspected, what was their response?

We were then told that the doctor had left for the day and that our concerns would be investigated the next morning. This is when I asked the nurse to get the doctor back on the phone because we were not leaving until someone looked into the infection. Ten minutes later, the nurse told us she'd spoken with another doctor and a CT scan was ordered. Results from that scan is what caused them to prep Shawnise for emergency exploratory surgery.

Exploratory surgery? What made them choose surgery?

They didn't know what was going on.

At first, they were going to wait until the next morning.

But when it became clear that her fever was not under control, and they saw fecal material on the CT scan it was decided the surgery had to be done right away.

Thank God a second opinion was consulted because it was then that they realized the need to go back in, find what was wrong, and fix it.

Unfortunately, by the time they did, it was too late. The damage had already been done.

What do you mean the damage had already been done?

Six days went by before anything was done about her infection. And at that point, I don't think what ended up happening could have been reversed even if they tried.

It was too late.

If we had known she had an infection earlier, the surgery and medicines could have prevented a lot of what happened.

It was like a domino effect. The infection went unchecked for so long that it caused kidney failure, collapsed lungs, respiratory failure, and congestive heart failure. And that's just a few things that Shawnise experienced because of that infection.

What do you think happened?

I think there was an error made. And that happens. But my daughter must be compensated. Her entire life has been changed. She cannot do the things she used to do or even would have done because of this.

It was wrong, and an effort needs to be made to make it right.

My daughter didn't do anything wrong, but she is the one paying the cost for what did go wrong.

I know Shawnise complained. Why do you think her complaints weren't investigated?

I don't really know why. Maybe it was because she was female. Maybe it was because she was a black woman.

When she first started complaining, they put a NG Tube down her throat hoping it would relieve gas or decomposition.

In addition to complaining, she was also fainting and having a fever. So the evidence that something was wrong was there – but nothing was done until the sixth day.

By then, we were all complaining, asking questions, and insisting that *something* be done.

It was clear that her health was declining fast!

How did you find out she had coded?

Shawnise was scheduled to go home. We were all excited. The day before she was discharged, I brought the baby to see her. Her aunts came. We were celebrating.

So, later that evening, when her sister (my oldest daughter) called me telling me that Shawnise had coded, I couldn't believe it.

She said she had just left the hospital and was about to get out of her car when her phone rang. The hospital called to tell her she needed to get back up there because Shawnise had coded.

How do you go from being excited and happy to go home to coding? What happened?

It just didn't make sense.

I believe the things we go through can help make us stronger and grow us. What do you think this experience has taught you?

I know God brought her back for a reason. And I don't think she can keep this to herself. This book is her testimony. Twenty minutes is a long time to be dead, but God brought her back.

He could have taken her and kept her, but He didn't.

And while she does have some lingering effects, she is in her right mind and can communicate. So that's why I know she must tell this story.

Why isn't testifying in church not enough?

Shawnise wants the world to know what happened to her. She could have just stopped with telling it in church. But our church is a small, family church.

This message is big.

Writing this book can go places she may not be able to go.

To be honest, we know that there are some people who went through what she did but didn't make it. They can't tell the story, but Shawnise can.

She was spared to tell her story! God has something in store for her.

What are some things that have happened since she decided to tell her story?

Not only has this impacted my daughter's life physically and emotionally, but as a mom, she missed bonding time with her baby. She can't get that back, and it hurts.

But thank God, she could pick up where she left off.

And after all she went through; she got a blessing in a healthy baby girl.

What does your daughter's life look like now?

Shawnise went from a healthy, carefree, and active young woman to a person who now fears life. She is in constant pain. She has healed on the outside, but there is still physical and emotional pain inside.

I see her wince even when her children jump on her to show affection.

She can do some things now, but she is afraid because of all the things she's gone through and nearly dying.

I know this journey has been challenging on Shawnise, but it had to be hard on you all as well. Tell me about that.

We were right there with her both in the hospital and when she got out.

My amazing aunts were there when we couldn't be there. They were our eyes and ears, and they watched over Shawnise. So even though I couldn't be there because of work, I never worried because I knew she was in great hands.

We stayed in shifts and did what needed to be done to care for her and her three children.

The cords, tubes, and battery for the defibrillator were all things that we had to pay attention to. If the battery died – she could die, so we had to be vigilant in our efforts.

But you do what you must do for your child.

What do you say to the people who may doubt Shawnise's story?

We have medical records to back up everything that happened to my daughter. She also has an attorney who is advocating for her. I don't think he'd have taken this case if her claims were not supported.

Do you have parting words for Shawnise's supporters?

After Shawnise's surgery, she had a wound vac. The wound looked like a deep gash, so she was very sore. When they changed the dressing Shawnise screamed and cried out for help. I saw they didn't give her anything to numb her.

I was angry. And I spoke up!

I let them know that they were not to touch her again until they gave her something for pain. They were not to hurt her unnecessarily.

If I hadn't been there – my daughter would have had to go through the pain she didn't need to go through.

My advice:

- Check on your loved ones. Be there for them.
- Educate yourself and be persistent in your complaints.
- Talk to the staff. It helps them see your loved ones as a person and not just a patient.
- Pray.

You don't know what is going on if you aren't there to see it. It's not just our children who need you, but also the elderly and sick – they all need someone to advocate for them.

As my daughter's story proves, prayer does change things.

***

Having her family there to watch over her, care for her, and advocate for her was God. Like them, I believe if she did not have them there, this would have been a different story – one that Shawnise may not have been around to tell.

Family is essential for many reasons.

Not the least of which is demonstrated by this family.

Sincere thanks to Shawnise and her family for allowing me the opportunity to play a small part in what I believe is a God-given assignment.

God bless you. The best is yet to come!

Iris M. Williams
Butterfly Typeface Publishing

God Within the Lily

Journal

The event that changed the direction of my life was my death. But death isn't the only thing that can bring about change.

Have you experienced a shift in your life?

If so, take a few days to reflect on it, write about it, and determine if the change in you has caused you to change.

Has the change been for the better?

One thing I've learned is that life is precious, and we must live it intentionally.

God is always speaking to us.

Are you listening?

Are you obeying?

God Within the Lily

Use the next few pages to journal your thoughts.
After some time, review what you've written.

Are there changes you need to make?

If so, don't wait.

Start living today!

God Within the Lily

Date: _____

God Within the Lily

Date: _____

God Within the Lily

Date: _____

God Within the Lily

Date: _____

God Within the Lily

Date: _____

God Within the Lily

Date: _____

God Within the Lily

Date: _____

God Within the Lily

Date: _____

God Within the Lily

Date: _____

God Within the Lily

Date: _____

Date: _____

Date: _____

Date: _____

Date: _____

Date: _____

God Within the Lily

Date: _____

God Within the Lily

Date: _____

Date: _____

God Within the Lily

Date: _____

God Within the Lily

Date: _____

God Within the Lily

Date: _____

Thank you

Praise for God Within the Lily

Shawnise, rarely have I have come across a kind soul as yours. You have inspired me and I'm sure many others. Strangers from far and near will feel emotions from your story. I am still in awe over your entire ordeal including your sickness, recovery, faith, recovery, and your ability to touch people by the strength you've demonstrated by fighting one illness after another. Your story is truly heartfelt and slowly brought a mist of sadness to my eyes and by the end of your words my tears were flowing. Although we are strangers, I felt sadness for you but only for a short time as I was reminded to slow down and remember that life really is only a "series of moments." Some will take these moments for granted. However, I will think of you when I'm feeling sorry for myself, when I feel like life is not going well or as I planned and remember to be grateful.

-Heidi Fairbanks

Shawnise, what an incredible encounter your near-death experience must have been! I loved reading all about it and envy your experience. You are a miracle, and you should keep sharing your story. People need to hear it. God bless you, dear heart, and may you continue to heal!

-Judy Kaelin

Shawnise, what a beautiful and inspirational story of survival. God obviously has plans for you. Deep peace and divine love.

-Mary Lou Bisinski

Shawnise: Far out! Now that's a story - one I feel will be relevant for many, many years.

-Elizabeth Fowkes

Shawnise, thank you for the courage it took to share your powerful and beautiful story.

-Cynthia Brink

Shawnise, I can't imagine the energy it cost for you to gather these experiences and write them out so eloquently for us to absorb. You're indeed a miracle and an inspiration.

-Janell Selkie Oelrich-Schreiber

Shawnise: Gosh, what a story! Harrowing and beautiful at the same time! Blessings to you and your lovely family.

-Laura Lian

Shawnise: Incredible! Thanks for sharing this beautiful and intriguing afterlife experience. I'm glad you came back to be with your girls. What beauties you all are.

-Samantha Lyons

Shawnise, you are a beautiful soul radiating an eternal love and light. You have such a precious heart. In my opinion you are exactly what this world so desperately needs. Thank you so much for sharing your experience!

-Olga Nan

Shawnise, I'm a retired nurse so my ears perked up when you spoke of your medical difficulties. They were many, enough for seven or more people! It's remarkable how you managed to get through all of that. You are a medical miracle, that's for sure. I hope you continue with improved health and spiritual growth.

-Susan Fanning

Shawnise, you really hung in there to live. You know you have a special mission here on earth. Peace to you always.

-Julie George

Shawnise, I was shocked by how many medical ailments you endured back-to-back. Talk about tribulations! But I LOVE your POSITIVE attitude despite it all. I also love that NDE inspires such beauty and emotion. Thank you for that session. The more I hear these 'Talking Flower' NDEs it makes me look at flowers in a whole new light. Maybe we should start talking to flowers! God Bless!

-Hajah Heals

We Make Good Great

www.butterflytypeface.com